Matter

See It, Touch It, Taste It, Smell It

Written by Darlene R. Stille
Illustrated by Sheree Boyd

Special thanks to our advisers for their expertise:

Paul Ohmann, Ph.D., Assistant Professor of Physics
University of St. Thomas, St. Paul, Minnesota

Susan Kesselring, M.A., Literacy Educator
Rosemount-Apple Valley-Eagan (Minnesota) School District

PICTURE WINDOW BOOKS
MINNEAPOLIS, MINNESOTA

Managing Editor: Bob Temple
Creative Director: Terri Foley
Editor: Nadia Higgins
Editorial Adviser: Andrea Cascardi
Copy Editor: Laurie Kahn
Designer: John Moldstad
Page production: Picture Window Books
The illustrations in this book were prepared digitally.

Picture Window Books
A Capstone Imprint
1710 Roe Crest Drive
North Mankato, MN 56003
www.capstonepub.com

Library of Congress Cataloging-in-Publication Data
Stille, Darlene R.
Matter : see it, touch it, taste it, smell it / written by Darlene Stille ;
illustrated by Sheree Boyd.
v. cm. — (Amazing science)
Includes bibliographical references and index.
Contents: What's matter?—Three kinds of matter—Changing states—
Describing matter—Be a solid scientist—Matters of fact.
ISBN 978-1-4048-0246-9 (library binding)
ISBN 978-1-4048-0344-2 (paperback)
1. Matter—Properties—Juvenile literature. [1. Matter—Properties.]
I. Boyd, Sheree, ill. II. Title. III. Series.
QC173.36 .S75 2004
530—dc22
                                                    2003016446

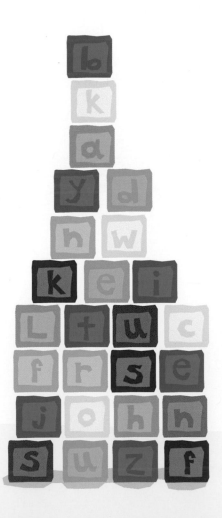

Table of Contents

What's Matter?

Can you see it? Can you touch it? Can you taste it? Can you smell it? If you can, it is made of matter.

FUN FACT

Even air is made of matter. Take a deep breath. You cannot see air. But you can feel air filling up your lungs.

4

Mountains, trees, and marshmallows all are made of matter. The stars in the sky are made of matter. Matter is anything that takes up space.

Look at a car. Look at a scooter. The car
is bigger and heavier than the scooter.
The car has more matter.

Things that have lots of matter are hard to move. It takes a strong grown-up to push a car, but you can push a scooter with just one foot.

FUN FACT

Things that have lots of matter are also hard to stop once they get moving. It is very hard to stop a train. It is easier to stop a car. It is very easy to stop a scooter.

Look at one of your hairs. See how thin it is? Imagine taking a strand of hair and slicing it into a million pieces. Each piece would be the size of the smallest bit of matter.

These tiny bits of matter are called atoms. Atoms are the building blocks of matter. They are much too small to see.

FUN FACT

Atoms fit together to make other building blocks called
molecules. Everything in the universe is made of atoms and
molecules. Billions of atoms and molecules make up the
matter in baseballs and rag dolls and you.

Three Kinds of Matter

Can you hold it? Does it bounce or stretch?
Does it feel hard, soft, or squishy?
It must be a solid.

There are three main kinds, or "states," of matter. Solids are one state of matter. Solids have shapes. A block of wood is a solid. An iron nail, a glass window, and a lump of clay all are solids.

Can you pour it? Does it spill? It must be a liquid. Liquids are another state of matter.

You cannot hold a liquid. A liquid runs through your fingers. It drips on the floor. A liquid does not have its own shape. A liquid has to be kept inside a container.

FUN FACT

A liquid takes the shape of what holds it. Look at a bottle of milk. Milk is a liquid. The milk has the shape of the bottle. Pour the milk into a glass. What shape does the milk have now?

13

Blow out some air through your mouth. Where did it go? Now blow some air into a balloon. Watch the balloon get bigger. The balloon holds the air.

14

The air around you is a gas. Gases are the third state of matter. A gas does not have a shape. You cannot pour a gas. A gas floats and spreads out in all directions. It completely fills whatever container it is in.

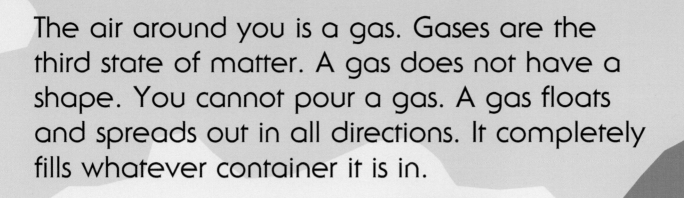

FUN FACT

The gas people put in their cars is different from gases such as air. That kind of gas is short for gasoline, a liquid fuel that gives cars energy to run.

Changing States

You now will turn a solid into a liquid.
Does this sound like a magic trick?

Take an ice cube out of the freezer.
Go outside, and put it in the sun.
Watch the solid ice turn to liquid water.

FUN FACT

The change from a solid to a liquid is called melting. Melting happens when a solid becomes hot enough. What happens to liquids when they get cold? What is that change called?

You now will see a liquid turn into a gas. Watch a kettle on a stove. The kettle is full of water. The burner on the stove makes the water very hot.

The hot water turns into a gas called steam.
The steam puffs out of the kettle's spout.
The steam makes the kettle whistle.

FUN FACT

Gases turn into liquids if they get cold enough. Look at the underside of a lid that has been used to cover a hot pot of soup. The lid is covered with drops of water. The steam from the soup cooled off and turned back into water.

Describing Matter

Look at the sky. What colors do you see?
Take a deep breath. What do you smell?
Dip your bare foot in the water. Is it cold?
Warm? We know one thing for sure—it's wet!

Color, smell, and feel are properties of matter.
You can name hundreds of properties that
describe all the wonderful matter in your world.

A rock and a pillow are both solids, but you can tell the difference. How? How many ways can you tell the difference between wood and glass? Milk and water?

21

Be a Solid Scientist

What you need:

Solids: Equipment:
a piece of wood   a pencil and paper
a nail   a wooden board about two feet (61 centimeters) long
a sheet of paper   a hammer
a stone   a bowl of water
aluminum foil
a lump of clay
a cork
a teaspoon of table salt
a feather from a pillow

What you do:
First, make a chart to organize your notes as you perform the following tests. List the names of the solids down the left side of the chart. Write these properties across the top: *hard, soft, stretches, tears, bends, breaks, floats.* As you do the following tests, put an X in the square if the solid has that property. You will be able to see at a glance the properties of the solids you tested.

Test #1: Is It Hard or Soft?
Place each solid on the board one at a time. With a grown-up's help, hit each solid with the hammer. What happens? Decide whether each item is hard or soft. Fill in your chart as you test each one.

Test #2: Does It Stretch or Tear?
Pick up and pull on each item. Which ones stretch and which ones tear? Record what happens.

Test #3: Can You Bend or Break It?
Try to bend each object. What happens to the paper? What happens to the foil? What happens to the lump of clay? Do any of these objects stay bent? Do any of the objects break in half? Record in the chart if the item bends or breaks.

Test #4: Will It Float?
One by one, place each item in the bowl of water. Which ones float? Complete your chart.

Matters of Fact

Lighter Than Air
Some gases weigh more than others. That's why a balloon filled with helium floats away when you let go of the string. Helium is lighter than the air around it.

No Matter
A space with no matter is called a vacuum. You make a kind of vacuum when you suck on a straw inside a glass of lemonade. Sucking takes the air out of the top of the straw. Matter always rushes in to fill a vacuum. That is why your drink climbs up the straw.

Feathers and Nails
A pillow takes up a lot more room than a box of nails. But the box of nails weighs more than the pillow. Why? The matter in the pillow is packed very loosely. The matter in the nails is packed more tightly. How tightly matter is packed in an object is called the object's density.

Melt or Burn?
When ice gets hot enough, it melts and becomes water. When wood gets hot enough, it burns and becomes ash. Water can change back into ice if it gets cold enough, but ash can never change back into wood. Heat makes matter change in different ways.

Smelly Matter
Why can you smell dinner cooking? Because little bits of matter from the food go into the air. Molecules from the food get in your nose. You can't see molecules, but you can smell them.

Melted Rocks
Many solids can turn into liquids if they get hot enough.
Rock melts in the deep, hot parts of the earth.
Melted rock pours out of a volcano like a river of fire.

Glossary

atom—the smallest bit of matter. Atoms are too tiny to see.
gas—a kind of matter that spreads to completely fill its container, such as air in a balloon
liquid—matter that is wet and can be poured, such as water
matter—anything that takes up space
molecule—a building block of matter that is made up of two or more atoms
solid—matter that has its own shape, such as glass or wood

To Learn More

More Books to Read

Mellet, Peter. *Matter and Materials*. New York: Kingfisher, 2001.

Simon, Charnan. *Solids, Liquids, Gases*. Minneapolis: Compass Point Books, 2001.

Snedden, Robert. *States of Matter*. Chicago: Heinemann Library, 2001.

Tocci, Salvatore. *Experiments with Solids, Liquids, and Gases*. New York: Children's Press, 2001.

Zoehfeld, Kathleen Weidner. *What Is the World Made Of? All About Solids, Liquids, and Gases*. New York: HarperCollins Publishers, 1998.

On the Web

FactHound offers a safe, fun way to find Web sites related to topics in this book. All of the sites on Fact Hound have been researched by our staff.

1. Visit *www.facthound.com*
2. Type in this special code: 1404802460
3. Click on the FETCH IT button.

Your trusty FactHound will fetch the best sites for you!

Index